AuthorHouse™
1663 Liberty Drive, Suite 200
Bloomington, IN 47403
www.authorhouse.com
Phone: 1-800-839-8640

First published by AuthorHouse 2/21/2008

ISBN: 978-1-4343-6625-2 (sc)

Printed in the United States of America
Bloomington, Indiana

This book is printed on acid-free paper.

authorHOUSE®

To Know Her Is To Love Her

By Stephanie Anderson

This book is dedicated to
my Superman, Dawson—
I love you, Dawson
Three hand squeezes for you

&

Maegan, my little piggy!

Chapters

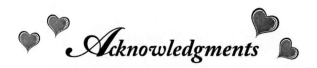

Acknowledgments

First and foremost, I want to thank God. He has made me who I am and I know now that I can do all things through Christ. I have praised Him through the storm and I could not have written this book without the many storms in my life.

To my children—

Maegan, my angel from God:
It has been a hard year away from you but I know time has allowed me to focus on this book. You have been in my heart and mind continually. You are an incredible daughter. I know that during your time away at college God will mold you into who He wants you to be. Trust Him through your steps in life and you will be great. I love you for who you are and not for what you do. Soar above the rest!

Dawson:
You have been a blessing to me this year. You have shown me a love I have never felt before. You have loved me so much and I feel so blessed to be your mother. You are an incredible kid and you will be a great kingdom builder someday. Love you with all my heart. — Mom.

Mom:
Mom you have taught me how to be a giver, how to be compassionate, how to love God and so many other things, I could not have written this book without Your Legacy!

To my sister Aline:
Where would we be without each other? Probably crazy .) :)
No, wait, we are crazy! LOL
I love that you and I have such a special bond. We can talk about anything and still love each other through the good and bad! You are truly my best friend! I can't imagine you not in my life. I need ya forever! I Love ya, sis!

To my Grandparents—
First, to my Grandpa Johnny:
I miss you but I know I will see you someday in heaven. Thank you for loving me so much as a kid. I could always talk you out of a dollar but I knew you loved giving it to me. I hope I have made you proud.

Papa Leroy:
I have loved you like my own Grandpa all my life. You are so special to me. I know I don't see you much but I think of you often.

Grandma Billy:
Time has separated us but I will always have the memories of being a kid at your house. I will never forget the time I ruined your new table with fingernail polish remover and all you said was, "It's okay, Honey. It's just a table." I love you.

To my friends and my clients—
Thank you for listening to me. I know I changed the style and name of this book a million times but you always smiled and said it was great. Thank you for believing in me.

Sabra & Jerry:
I am so thankful to be back in your lives. I am so proud of both of you: Jerryaudley.com for your amazing talent, Sabra for your drive and passion to help others. You are so strong and I know someday it will pay off for both of ya! I love y'all!

Sherrie & Susan:
Thank you for your brilliance in design and editing. You two made this book come alive!

Joe: ❤
My true Love! I feel so blessed to have you in my life. I have smiled everyday since the day you came into my life! You complete me in every way! I love everything about you. I love your smile, I love your heart, and I love the way you make me feel! I love your family; they have been so kind to me! Thank you for all that you do for me! I promise to always love and honor you!

Kathey & Andy:
Thank you for raising an amazing son! Thank you for welcoming me into your family with open arms. I have loved every minute! Even the teasing from you, Andy! I promise to love and honor Joe forever!

Samantha & Shelby:
I have truly loved getting to know you two! You are beautiful and talented girls! You both have so much to offer. You both are so unique and I love that about you! Stay strong and always follow your dreams!

To the rest of Joe's family — Aunt Judy, Aunt Joyce, Jeff, Joanna & Gus — thank you for your kindness!

I have a passion to help ignite excitement in couples all over America and when you have a passion it will push you to do things you never would have done before (such as writing a book).

$\mathcal{I}$ntroduction

This book will be one of the greatest tools
you will ever possess in your relationship.
For men, it will teach how to:

- 💜 Plan the perfect night
- 💜 Surprise her with Love Ideas
- 💜 Ignite a newfound passion you did not know existed
- 💜 Open up a whole new world of love and fulfillment

For women, it will give a place to record what's important to you
and your relationship.

I wrote this book because I think it is important for couples to know
and experience each other in every area of their lives. It is no secret
that men often tend to forget — as well as have more difficulty
remembering — important dates and special times that are precious to
women's hearts.

One of the first questions that people ask when I talk about my
concept for *To Know Her is To Love Her* is, "What gave you the

idea?" This inspiring idea emerged from an overwhelming desire to teach and help couples draw closer together. It comes from thinking about how wonderful it would be to have a place where all types of information about each other could be available at a moment's notice, such as:

- Likes
- Dislikes
- Ring size
- Shoe size
- Wish list
- ❤ ❤ ❤ and much more.

All this information could be kept in a journal of sorts, and in one place, somewhat like *CliffsNotes* for couples, or cheat sheets for men.

One afternoon after my divorce, I was thinking about it and wondering, "How can I help couples stay connected? How could I help end divorces? What can I do to prevent a future divorce in my own life?"

After thinking about the last sixteen years of my marriage, I wondered what could have made a difference? What could have kept me from a divorce? I've always believed the adage, "Failure is *success* if you learn from it."

Two of the big things that I found along this journey and pathway:
1. He did not know me, and
2. Like many women, I always assumed he could read my mind, or I wanted him to.

I believe that had this book been available to me, I would not be a divorced woman right now. My marriage would have been spared.

Knowledge leads to intimacy for couples and your key to opening that lock lies within the pages of this book. Let me explain a little bit more about the creative beginnings of *To Know Me is To Love Me*.

It was approximately twelve years into my sixteen-year marriage when all hell broke loose. My husband was going out for sandwiches. He was gathering orders for the family when he came to me and said, "What kind of sandwich do you want?"

I laughed and said, "You are kidding, right?"

He looked puzzled and said, "No, what kind?"

"A ham-and-cheese foot-long," I said. "We always share that."

"Okay, and what do you want on it?" he asked.

"The same as I have ordered for twelve years," I said.

"What is that?" he asked.

Here is the kicker of the story. He asked if I wanted mayo or mustard. I hate mustard!

Okay, so right now you're thinking, she divorced him over mustard? No, that was the straw, or combination of things, that broke the camel's back and at this point I no longer wanted the sandwich or was even hungry — just angry.

I said, "No, what I do want is for you to know me. After twelve years, why should I have to tell you what kind of sandwich I like? I mean, if you really loved me, you would know me."

Right? Not exactly. You see, men simply don't store that kind of information. It does not compute. They just don't get it. Help is needed and help is here.

This is where *To Know Her is To Love Her* comes into the picture. She will have written down all her hidden secrets and desires to share with you; all you have to do is read.

Had my ex had this book, he could have ordered everything just the way I like it, without asking, and let me know he loved me at the same time. Brilliant!

Men, let me share some inside secrets to a woman's soul. We need you to make us feel that we are all *that* and so much more! (Snap, snap, snap!) Crazy as it sounds, it is true. We want to be Mrs. One-and-Only, now and forever more.

Yes, of course, it will take time and discipline to accomplish, however, oh my, what a great treasure awaits you at the end of this book!

You will learn to get up-close and personal with the woman who loves you, and you will discover again the love dancing that brought you together, along with her likes and dislikes.

This book will be priceless to your future love life!

I don't believe anyone gets married expecting to just exist in a state of boredom. We all want to have that original loving feeling sustain us through the years. Problems develop if we allow ourselves to get into a rut of despair and are unable to function, or put any effort into our man or marriage; everything begins to disintegrate.

Have you heard women say (over and over again), "What I want is for him to know me without me having to explain what I want."

Women need to realize that men simply don't notice the importance of these issues on their own; therefore, we must teach them what we need. Think of the countless hours of arguing gone out the window once you have your hands on the information in this book.

You will find loads of options and opportunities to get organized and begin your new journey of communication.

Your man still has to pick one of the 20 or more choices you have given him and it will still be a surprise when he plans the date, but how sweet and thoughtful and tons of fun this is going to be, knowing he took the time to search out the information and create a special time just for you.

Men, it is time to step up to the challenge of knowing what is on her mind and how she likes it. You will be greatly rewarded with a personalized date night. Trust me, if you learn the key to her happiness, you will love the rewards.

(Women, don't forget to pick up a copy of *To Know Him is To Love Him* so you can rock his world.)

"Don't assume he can read your mind!"

To Know Her
Is To *Love* Her

To Know Her is to Love Her was created to help you as a man learn how to know her thoughts and to have access to those thoughts at any given moment.

How, you ask? It's simple!

The format of this book provides you with user-friendly, goof-proof, power tools to make a good quality decision for any special occasion or date event.

Your partner is going to fill in all her favorite restaurants, a wish list, shoe size, and even her ring size. You will soon discover her likes and dislikes and have a vast array of information about her. This information will enable you to plan a night of romance or adventure and be right on target as to what she needs to create a unique time together.

No more guessing! Gone are the hurt feelings of rejection that drive a wedge between the two of you. Now you have the opportunity to sweep her off her feet with confidence about the outcome.

Let me talk to her for a minute.

I recommend picking up several copies of this book because you need one in his car, one at his work place, and perhaps one in your bathroom. (Think about it. The bathroom may be the only place you can get him to read it!)

Consider this: if your prince is out and about at your favorite mall and there is a diamond sale happening, trust me, girlfriend, you are going to want him to have your ring size available for the perfect fit.

When he goes to your favorites section of the book, no guessing will be required as that information will be readily available. He will know if you like diamonds or pearls, gold or silver, rubies or topaz. It doesn't matter how pretty the ring is, you won't wear it as happily if he buys silver and you love gold.

I am giving him the opportunity to be able to plan the perfect night. I know you think, "Shut up, girlfriend. You don't know my husband." Actually, I don't need to know your husband. I have designed this all for you.

This book contains valuable information to enhance, revive, and stir up your relationship, along with simple ideas to find each other again.

It's this simple to plan a date night: in the address section under babysitters you will write the information he needs and with a flip of his wrist he could plan an amazing evening for the two of you. Give him some time, have some tender patience, and teach him

12

everything about you and who you are. Before you know it, he will be sweeping you off your feet.

There are a lot of great books out there on relationships and I have read my share of them. But something was missing in most of them. They offered great ideas, but usually only about 25 percent of any such book worked for me. That is what makes this book different and unique. *To Know Her is To Love Her* is designed just for you!

You have heard the saying, "It's the thought that counts." Let me rephrase that for couples: "It's *knowing* her thoughts that counts."

For example, I love milk chocolate and hate dark chocolate. How do you suppose I would feel if someone gave me dark chocolate? Not too special, obviously. I would kindly thank someone for such a gift and in the trash it would go. But if someone gave me milk chocolate, I would feel special because they took the time to know me.

Men, how many times have you been in the doghouse because you bought the wrong gift or sent the wrong flowers?

From now on she will feel like "He knows me and he loves me." Women need to feel loved and know they are loved. And the little things are important, even down to whether your lady likes mustard or mayonnaise on her foot-long ham-and-cheese sandwich.

As I described in the Introduction, I felt so sad that after so many years my husband had never taken the time to know what I liked. To him it was no big deal whether I liked mayonnaise or mustard, and (have you heard this before?) he said I was overreacting.

This became a running joke in my family, but to me it was a wound that never healed. I wanted him to know me because *To Know Me is To Love Me!*

Men, how many Brownie points can you muster up in a day? It is endless: make a phone call just to say "I am thinking of you," or leave a love note for her to find on the bathroom mirror. It is so simple. You want a happy home sharing the most intimate parts of your life together? This connection is possible and will happen if you just put forth a little effort.

A woman wants to feel that you have eyes only for her and that she is queen of the house. And that could come from something as simple as knowing if she likes mayo or mustard.

Thus the need for cheat sheets to help you remember not only the little things, but help in the problem areas. As one man said to me, "When she mentions something she wants, I have no place to write it down, and then when her birthday comes, I can't for the life of me remember what she said. I mean, who can remember a conversation that may have happened months ago?"

Think of it, no more lost gift ideas. You will now have a place to store all that information and when you hear her say, "Boy, I would like a massage," or, "I need my hair done," you can run to your book, and make an appointment for her to have a massage and/or hair appointment.

By now you could be thinking, "Hey, what's in it for me?" Have no fear. She will also own a copy of *To Know Him is To Love Him* with all the information you have filled out about what makes you feel special and loved.

14

Remember, to love me is to know me!

You may think she already knows you, but does she really?

💜 Could she call your best friend and book a tee time at your favorite course?

💜 Buy the latest hunting gear that you don't have?

"I love milk chocolate!"

"My favoriate clor is pink!"

"I love Gerbera daisies!"

♥ Or know whether you'd prefer tickets to a hockey game or a rock concert?

My friend was once asked to give her husband's height and exact weight to pre-order snow skis for a winter trip and realized that she was guessing.

See, you didn't think you could benefit so much from *To Know Him is To Love Him.* But think again. Make it happen. So much closeness and intimacy will be at your fingertips just by opening up to sharing your favorite things.

Don't forget to include your favorite love spots and massage areas. Trust me, this book has great fringe benefits.

What good is a great date idea if it doesn't apply to you? Her favorite night out might be dinner and a movie, but yours is a home-cooked meal and a little love dancing (if you know what I mean).

Look through the exceptional Great Date ideas to add to her favorites or to spark a little creativity. You will also find all kinds of Love Notes and Love Coupons to leave for her.

You will soon learn the pleasures of listening to her and writing things down.

You will come to love this book. It will keep you out of the doghouse and no more eating doggy bones!

Listen to her and keep a copy of *To Know Her is To Love Her* around the house, in the car, and at the office. When she calls to say, "Honey, the kids are driving me crazy," you will know just what to do to soothe her. You will hold the key to her heart while she holds the key to yours.

"In *Real Love* You Want The Other Person's Good,

In *Romantic Love* You Want The Other Person!"

Margaret Anderson

Love Ideas

Do you need some spice in your relationship, or are you bored? Well this section's for you. Love ideas will add some spice to your life. They are different from date ideas and most are very inexpensive and only take time, thought, and love.

Just take these ideas and have her pick her top 20. Ask her often to update it so you will have new ideas to pick from and always have her write in pencil so she can keep the new ideas coming. Tell her if she has some other ideas that she thinks would be nice have her write her own.

If you are short on money, print her a picture or description of virtually anything and tell her that if you could you would buy her the world.

This is my favorite chapter. To me this is the chapter that sparks Love Dancing 101.

I hope this chapter will ignite a new passion and excitement that's probably been missing in your relationship for a long time.

The more you use this chapter the better you will get. You will be a love expert in no time.

Learn to be creative, think outside the box. Personalize things as often as you can. Everybody loves their name so when you leave her a special note write her name for example. _____ let's kiss and make up, Trust me it will make her tingle.

Remember to always honor her. Never, I mean never, criticize her. Men, this is so important. Your words have the power of life and death. Your words can kill a marriage. You can destroy a night by one negative comment. Honor her and she will honor you.

Never use sex as a bargaining tool. Women don't think of sex the same way that men do. Women tend to think that's all men care about. I know you are probably saying that's true. Just because you do something special for her, don't expect her to do something in return for you.

To a woman, love and respect come from outside the bedroom. For men it comes from inside the bedroom. When you respect her outside the bedroom, she will learn to respect you in the bedroom.

Before long, you will be doing some amazing love dancing.

Give her a copy of *To Know Him is to Love Him* (coming 2008). There are some great sexy suggestions for her to ignite a new love passion in this book.

Love Ideas to Try

Slip a ring on her finger while she sleeps.
    Or
A new bracelet.
    Or
Skinny dip in your pool.
    Or
Ask your mate to take a shower with you.
    Or
Make a list about what you find sexy about her.
    Or
What attracted you to her?
    Or
Have her meet you outside in the winter for a snuggle with coffee, tea or (say) me.
    Or
Send pizza to the office for her birthday. (What is her favorite pizza?)
    Or
Cater dinner from her favorite restaurant. (What is her favorite restaurant?)
    Or
Meet for coffee before work. (Favorite coffee: iced or hot?)
    Or
Meet for breakfast like you're dating.
    Or
Give her a pedicure.
    Or
Massage her feet.
    Or
Go to a foreign film.

Or

Snuggle and smooch in the back of the movies.

Or

Set your room up for a massage.

Or

A romantic night with roses, candles, melted chocolate and fruit.

Or

Make breakfast in bed for her.

Or

Surprise her for lunch.

Or

Stay in a suite and act like newlyweds.

Or

Stay at the hotel and act like kings and queens; order room service and get a massage.

Or

Tuck love notes in her sock drawer.

Or

Go to the park and swing.

Or

Send her an invitation for a Royal night out.

Or

A royal night in.

Or

Leave hidden notes for her.

Or

Place them in drawers.

Or

Leave a note in the shower.

Or

Text her a love message.

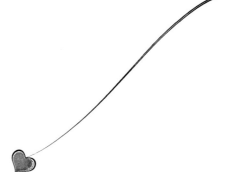

Or

Sneak a gift in her car. (See wish list)

Or

Feed the kids first.

Or

Set up a table in the other room for the two of you.

Or

Make a love chain 30 days before your anniversary with compliments on each link.

It's not the thought that counts,
it's knowing her thoughts that count!

Or

The month before her birthday.

Or

Drive around with a "Just Married" sign.

Or

Been married night out.

Or

Create a compliment book.

Or

A compliment jar.

Or

Play truth or dare.

Or

Strip checkers.

Or

Send flowers with a thoughtful note.

Or

Hand deliver.

Or

Put candles all over the house.

Or

All over the bedroom.

Or

Write a love poem.

Or

Love note.

Or

Have a love sign made.

Or

Advertise on a blown up balloon.

Or

Create a web page just for her.

Or

Have her favorite saying framed.

Or

Create a new saying for the two of you.

Or

Send an edible arrangement.

Or

Cookie bouquet.

Or

Buy her a goldfish.

Or

Build her a water garden.

Or

Record her favorite song. (What is her favorite song?)

Or

Sign her up on her favorite bands' fan site.
(Who is her favorite band?)

Or

Hire a professional to hang Christmas lights.
    Or
Do it yourself.
    Or
Hire someone to organize her closet.
    Or
Have the house cleaned.
    Or
Create a love bowl with compliments.
    Or
Love ideas.
    Or
Find a family saying that leaves a legacy.
    Or
A family event that is remembered for a life time.
    Or
Buy some Legos
    Or
Lincoln Logs and build together.
    Or
Create your own Love stamp.
    Or
 Buy some love stickers.
    Or
Make your own candles. (What's her favorite scent?)
    Or
Soap together.
    Or
Dance in the rain.
    Or
Just dance anywhere.
    Or
 Go for a walk.

Rollerblade. (Buy her some. What's her shoe size?)
    Or
Make a cake together. (What's her favorite flavor?)
    Or
Make hot sauce together (Hot or mild?)
    Or
Send her an e-mail of different jewelry items and tell her to pick one.
    Or
 Send her a catalog and tell her to put hearts around her favorites.

Words Can Last A Lifetime!

    Or
Have a chick flick marathon. (See favorite movie list)
    Or
Serve her dinner in bed. (What is her favorite dinner?)
    Or
Lunch in bed.
    Or
Buy a charm bracelet for her and give her a charm a day for a week.
    Or
A month.
    Or
Leave rose petals in unexpected places, wrapped in a towel
    Or
Floating in the toilet.

Make a love box.

Or

Use a mailbox.

Or

Watch the sunrise together.

Or

The sunset.

Or

Run her bath water. (Find out if she likes bubbles or no bubbles, wine or music?)

Or

Warm her towel.

Or

Fill unexpected places with balloons (behind the shower curtain or in a closet).

Or

In the trunk of her car.

Or

Have a pillow fight.

Or

Just tickle her.

Or

Buy a heart-shaped pancake maker.

Or

A heart-shaped cookie cutter.

Or

Text a love message.

Or

E-mail a love message.

Or

Scan a picture of the two of you and have it transferred to a pillow.

Or

Scan a vacation scene and transfer it to a pillow.

Or

Clean the house for her.

Or

Give her a 30 minute break from the kids.

Or

Give her a day of heart-shaped food and give her a heart charm.

Or

Cut heart shapes in pictures and love notes.

Or

Give her a bath basket; pack it with all kinds of goodies such as candles, a robe, a boat.

Or

A rubber ducky with a note; remember what it was like to relax and be a kid again.

Or

Send index cards to all her friends and family asking them to write compliments

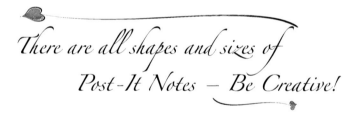

There are all shapes and sizes of Post-It Notes – Be Creative!

Or

What they admire most about her.

Or

Give her a basket of gifts such as candles and candleholders.

A basket full of great coffees along with a new mug.

Or

A basket of tea with a note that says, "Here, have some T (ea)LC."

Or

Give her a basket full of mirrors, all shapes and sizes, with
a note that says, "You are more beautiful than the first time
I saw you."

Or

Create a recipe love box in the kitchen so when she's cooking
she can always pick one to look at.

Or

For her birthday give her a gift for each letter of her name.

Or

For Christmas.

Or

Give her some new perfume with a note that says she was
heaven scent.

Or

Celebrate her half-birthday.

Or

When you have had a fight leave a note near her lipstick that
says lets kiss and make up.

Or

Give her a subscription to her favorite magazine.

Or

When she compliments you

Or

Gives you encouragement; leave her a handful of mints and tell
her thanks for the compliment and encouragement.

Or

On a Friday night bring home a basket full of movie stuff:
popcorn, candy, and soda pop.

Or

Give her all kinds of note pads. (Hint: she will leave you lots
of love notes.)

Or

Give her a gift certificate to her favorite spa with a note that says you are spectacular.

Or

Start a friendship journal to pass back and forth: write; "Tag, you're it."

Or

Start a love journal.

Or

Give her a box of chocolates with a piece of jewelry hidden inside.

Or

A stuffed puppy with a jewelry dog tag that's a new bracelet.

Leave a CD in her car with songs such as, "I just called to say I love you."

Or

An old favorite song that brings back memories.

Create a special way to tell her you love her like a handshake.

Or

A special wink.

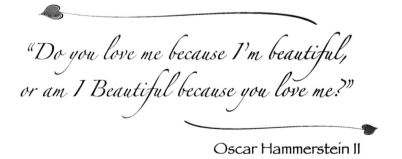

"Do you love me because I'm beautiful,
or am I Beautiful because you love me?"

Oscar Hammerstein II

Write Your Top Love Ideas For Him
Use pencil to make your list and update it often

1. _____

2. _____

3. _____

4. _____

5. _____

6. _____

7. _____

8. _____

9. _____

10. _____

11. _____

12. _____

13. _____

14. _____

15. _____

16. _____

17. _____

18. _____

19. _____

20. _____

Great Date Ideas

Okay guys, by now you know the drill. The key to this chapter and book is to make her feel special.

Men, here's your chance to sweep her off her feet. Be creative, take a look at her top date choices for inspiration and sweep her off her feet.

Be spontaneous. Take her for a walk. Hold her hand. Show her how much she means to you. Surprise her often, so she will feel special.

Try to plan at least two dates a month. It will ignite a new atmosphere in your relationship.

Keep the babysitter's number on hand. When you or she has a bad day and need a night out, you can plan the night without any help from her. She will love you for this. A no-stress date, that's the best. It allows her time to prepare herself for you. Blame it on Hollywood but women love a man who can plan the perfect evening.

Do you ever wonder what women see in a chick flick? Let me share some inside secrets. It's all about the romance and making her tingle inside, feeling like she is the only one in your eyes.

Women love to feel like the queen, a superstar.

Women can be confusing because we act like we don't care but deep down we want our men to read our minds and sweep us off our feet.

In this chapter you will learn how to plan the perfect date and how to sweep her off her feet.

Have her write her top 20 date ideas and then you plan the night. You can't go wrong because she picked them.

Pay attention if she says dinner and a movie. Know her top restaurants. If it's Mexican, know which Mexican restaurant? We may all love Mexican, but we all have a favorite Mexican restaurant. So don't just settle for the one closest to the house.

How much easier can it get?

All the information is here so you will become her Hollywood stud before you know it.

This book is designed so you don't have to read her mind anymore. The goal is to eventually Know her so well you will only have to look in this book for sizes and wish list.

You will be her stud, her dreamboat, her night in shining armor.

Don't forget when planning a date:

- ❤ Call the babysitter or in-laws.
- ❤ Leave her a Love note in the morning to start the day off right.
- ❤ Try to do a Love idea before or after the date.
- ❤ Go above and beyond when it's your turn. Make it special!

Examples:
For a night out:

- ❤ Call babysitter
- ❤ Call restaurant
- ❤ Make after-dinner plans
- ❤ Suggestions: Treat her with flowers, a new outfit, massage, hair styling, manicure or pedicure.

For a night in:

- ❤ Call babysitter
- ❤ Order food or do the cooking
- ❤ Plan a movie
- ❤ Plan something special to show her your love for her.

Date Ideas to Try

1. Stay in a hotel; order room service.

2. Find a dance studio that will give private lessons.

3. Meet for breakfast and act like you're dating.

4. Surprise each other by meeting at work for lunch.

5. Hire a dance instructor to come to your house.

6. Stay in a hotel suite and act like newlyweds.

7. Have a romantic night with candles, chocolate, and fruit. (Light chocolate or dark, and what's her favorite fruit?)

8. Go to the movies and smooch like you're teenagers.

9. Meet for coffee. (Order in advance. What's her favorite?)

10. Go to a foreign film.

11. Recreate your first date. (Do you remember what it was?)

12. Set up your room for a massage. (What's her favorite place to be massaged?)

13. Recreate your favorite date.

14. Find a park with a pond, have a picnic, and feed the ducks.

15. Create a love web page for the two of you.

16. Play bingo.

17. Celebrate her half birthday. (Make her favorite cake.)

18. Take a ceramics class together.

19. Take scuba lessons together. (See Yellow Pages.)

20. Take a cooking class together. (Check local paper.)

21. Find a caricature artist and have him draw you together. (Check a local art school.)

22. Rent an RV and wrestle in the back seat.

23. Rent a limo.

24. Have a party and invite all her friends over. (Choose a theme.)

25. Rent a costume and plan a royal night in.

26. Buy a fondue pot and feed each other. Get creative. (Will it be white chocolate or milk chocolate?)

27. Rent a houseboat for the night. (What's her favorite lake? Check newspaper for rental possibilities.)

28. Fill up an air mattress and watch her favorite movie in the middle of the living room.

29. Make heart-shaped cookies with special love messages on them.

30. Put white butcher paper all over the kitchen and body paint each other with pudding; feed each other while blindfolded.

31. Visit a used bookstore. (Find her favorite childhood book.)

32. Advertise "I Love You" on an inflatable balloon.

33 Hire a band to play at your house while you have a romantic dinner. (What's her favorite music?)

34 Find a local campground and spend the night. (Check local Chamber of Commerce for tips.)

35 Select a local museum to visit. (Check local paper.)

36 Visit your local gardens. (Check local paper.)

37 Visit your local aquarium. (Check local paper.)

38 Visit a local theater (live or movie. Check local paper.)

39 Try sushi.

40 Try Thai food.

41 Try Brazilian food.

42 Try German food.

43 Try Indian food.

44 Take a dinner cruise.

45 Hire a horsedrawn carriage. (See wedding section in Yellow Pages.)

46 Join a gym together. Have a smoothie at the gym and make it romantic by sharing one straw. You might even bring candles. (Pack a romantic bag.)

Take her to get a new outfit or shoes. (See size chapter)

Play kid games such as Twister, hopscotch, or water balloons. Get out some Crayons and don't forget the marbles. (What is her favorite old game?)

Have a food fight with whipped cream and a cherry on top.

Buy a metal detector, hunt for treasures, and then frame your finds.

Go to a park with a pond. Bring floating candles and dessert.

Play miniature golf or go to an arcade. You might find an old favorite game such as Pac-Man.

Plan a festive evening at home with an exotic Mexican, Italian, Greek, Balinese, or Japanese theme and decorate your house to match.

Remember the little things when you go on vacation or the weekends. Treat her like royalty and go overboard on love notes, flowers, and back massages. Enjoy a royal nap together.

When you go to a restaurant, not only share your food, share the booth. Get close, be silly, feed each other. I am sure people will look at you with envy.

Who says you can't bring candles and a tablecloth to your favorite fast food restaurant?

Buy her a new piece of jewelry and slip it to the waitress at dinner to present it with dessert. Even a simple pair of earrings says you care. Trust me, it doesn't have to be expensive.

Most people love to dine outdoors. Plan your dinner outside and be creative. Hang strings of lights that are sexy and romantic, light candles, and put on the music.

Set up candles all over the house and when you think you have enough, add more. Add a few balloons... Sweep her off feet and she might sweep you off yours.

Remember how much fun you had as a kid at the park? Try it again. Swing, slide, run, play tag, throw a Frisbee. Bring the sidewalk chalk, carve your initials in a tree, fly a kite. Play in the sandbox and pretend you are at the beach and make a sand castle.

Go to the library and have a book hunt. Pre-select the books to find and meet back at the couch to share a love poem and read it to each other.

Plan a day of pictures in a photography studio and in the outdoors.

Go iceskating.

Go rollerskating.

Find a bear shop and build a bear; record a special message to place inside for her.

 *Women Love to Feel Special!*

Write Your Date Love Ideas For Him

Use pencil to make your list and update it often

1. _____

2. _____

3. _____

4. _____

5. _____

6. _____

7. _____

8. _____

9. _____

10. _____

11. _____

12. _____

13. _____

14. _____

15. _____

16. _____

17. _____

18. _____

19. _____

20. _____

Write Your Own Love Notes

This chapter is designed to help you write your own Love notes.

Go to a local office supply store and buy all shapes and sizes of Post-it Notes. If you haven't seen self-stick notes in a while, you will be surprised at all the variety. They come in all shapes and sizes, and any color you could want.

Leave her Love notes at least three times a week. Be creative. Take my ideas and expand on them. Add your own flair.

You may think once a week is enough for a love note but it's not.

Let me explain. You could leave her a love note, call her a couple of times during the day but just before you leave the office someone makes you mad. You come home and don't talk because you need some time to unwind.

Sensing your mood, she might go crazy thinking you don't love her or that you only called her and left her a note because you felt guilty. You may be saying, "That's crazy." This is where men don't understand women. Heck, we don't even understand ourselves. We change our mind every time we turn around.

Like you, women need encouragement. When you need time to yourself, kiss her and tell her how much you love her. Ask for some time to unwind, take your time, and then thank her for being understanding. This will work so much better than retreating into silence with no explanation.

 Love Note Ideas

1. Why don't you try and score a touchdown tonight?

2. Got some? Want some?

3. Have you scored a goal lately? How about scoring one on me!

4. I want you.

5. I'm sorry. Can we kiss and make up?

6. Just because I love you!

7. Love you a latte!

8. Just because you are special!

9. Take me. I'm yours!

10. I love you. I love your smile. I love the way you tease me. I love it when you whisper in my ear. I love the way you love me.

11. When I think about you, stuff tingles.

12. When I think about you, my heart beats like a thousand drums.

13. I would do anything for you.

14. You are my everything.

15. Want to make out?

16. For going above and beyond, thank you.

17. I love everything about you.

18. You are my favorite pillow.

19. You are my favorite hot spot.

20. Your love adds spice to my life.

21. I have written your name on my book of love in permanent marker.

22. You're one in a million for a million and one reasons.

23. You are hotter than a HEMI.

24. You are my favorite flavor.

You are the brightest star. I could spot you anywhere.

You melt better than chocolate.

You are my chocolate chip.

Oh, the things you do to me! When can you do them again?

I want you and I enjoy needing you.

Bring the "Do not disturb" sign.

Want to get frisky?

Love muffin, honey bun, cupcake, sweetie pie. You are my favorite treat.

You don't have a clue how SEXY you really are.

You are my angel.

I will always love you, honor you and adore you.

I love loving you.

You are my sunshine.

Everyday I fall in love with you again.

GRRRRRRRR

You are the love notes that complete my heart's song.

I just thought I couldn't love you more and then a new day comes and I hear a new song of love.

I am yours, all yours. Can you handle that?

I'm so blessed to have you to snuggle, cuddle, kiss, and hug with.

I'd brake for you.

You are the only scent I crave.

Let's take a ride on the wild side.

You mean more to me than you will ever know.

I wished upon a star and there you were.

Got love, need some, want some?

Do you want to date me?

I'd love to kiss you all over.

You are the wings that make me soar.

You're looking so good today.

You still have it and I still want it.

You complete me.

Just when life started to get dull, you added a rainbow of color to my life.

Do you like baseball? I'll let you run my bases.

Do you want to play doctor?

Let's double-dip tonight.

I would follow you down any road.

Remember always, you are loved.

You are the song my heart sings all day.

You can float your marshmallows in my hot chocolate anytime.

You are my Love Boat.

You are my superstar.

You can top my sundae anytime.

You are the love of my life.

You complete me.

My world got brighter the day you stepped into it.

I am glad you were my last first kiss.

Have I told you lately that you still take my breath away?

I love you more than the day we met.

You are more beautiful than any garden.

Every day that I wake up with you recharges my battery.

Write Your Top Love Note Suggestions

1. _____

2. _____

3. _____

4. _____

5. _____

6. _____

7. _____

8. _____

9. _____

10. _____

11. _____

12. _____

13. _____

14. _____

15. _____

16. _____

17. _____

18. _____

19. _____

20. _____

Write Your Own Love Coupons

Just like writing your own love notes, you can write your own love coupons.

Try to print some of these on your computer. Personalize them whenever you can for something that you know she will like. Write her name on them. It will make her feel like you really care when it is written just for her.

Be respectful. Honor her with the coupons. Never treat her like she owes you something in return. Make her feel special with these coupons. Never give expecting something in return. Women know when you are giving just to receive.

When you learn to give from your heart, you will receive the greatest reward. (How about some of the best love dancing you have ever had?)

This coupon is good for

A Royal Night Out

Redeemable: TONIGHT   Love,
                              ME

Love Coupon Ideas

This coupon is good for:

A royal night out.

A royal night in.

A nail appointment.

A day of beauty.

A candlelight bath.

A free dishwashing.

TV all to yourself.

Respect Comes from Outside the Bedroom!

Your turn to pick the movie.

A day to yourself.

A massage for___minutes.

A love touch anywhere you would like.

A morning to sleep in.

A nap anytime you need it.

Dinner in bed.

Breakfast in bed.

A day of shopping.

You to be "Queen for the day."

A trip to the outlet mall.

Your choice of date idea or love idea.

A three-wish day.

A weekend away of your choice.

How to
Know Me . . .

This is the beginning of the chapters that will be all about her — the true gold in this book. These next chapters will be like finding the key to the treasure chest of you relationship. You will unlock a treasure in her that will be beyond your wildest dreams.

Remember, to know her is to love her. So begin by studying these chapters. Keep this information in your mind as you learn her favorites. Learn her sizes. Know if she likes mayo or mustard.

And keep a copy of *To Know Her is to Love Her* where you can find it!

The Basics

My birthday/ birthstone _____

Anniversary _____

Special day _____

Important Names and Numbers
- Florist_____
- Ticketmaster_____
- Hair Salon _____
- Nail Salon _____
- Massage _____
- Tanning Salon _____

Favorite Stores
- Clothes _____
  _____
- Shoes_____
- Jewelry (gold or silver, diamonds or pearls?)_____
  _____
- Home accessories_____

Treats

- Magazine _____
- Candy_____
- Soda _____
- Coffee_____
- Pizza _____
- Take-out _____

Necklace length _____

Watch _____

Shirt sizes:
♥ Short sleeve _____

♥ Button-up _____

♥ T-shirt _____

Pants size _____

Shorts size _____

Capri size _____

Sweats size _____

Shoe Size
♥ High heels _____

♥ Tennis shoes _____

♥ Boots _____

Bra size/favorite brand _____

Panty size _____

- ♥ Dinner _____
- ♥ Pie _____
- ♥ Cake _____

My Sizes

Have her go to a local jeweler to determine her ring size. Tell her to be specific. Have her measure both her right and left hands. Have her measure her wrist size, so you can have that watch or bracelet sized before you give it to her.

Once you have this information remember to use it. Make sure it is the right size before you give it to her and if it's not right, make it right.

I remember once when my ex bought me a bracelet in the airport and they only had a large size so he bought it anyway. He gave it to me and said, "You will have to send it off to have it sized." I remember thinking, "How thoughtless of him. Buying me a gift just to say he did and then telling me to send it off."

I left the bracelet on the counter with the jeweler's address, determined not to have it sized or sent off. I thought, "Why should I have to send it off? He should do it." Needless to say, I never sent it off and it never got done. The more I looked at that bracelet, the more I hated it. It reminded me of how much he cared, or didn't.

So remember, you hold the key —or diamond — to her happiness.

Ring size _____

Wrist measurement _____
56

I prefer:
Put a heart by or circle the one you love!

I Like ❤ ❤ ❤

Roses, daisies, orchids

Sweats or Shorts

Boxers or Briefs

T-shirt or Polo

Massage or Playful

Shoes or Purses

Belts or Socks

SUV or Sedan

Sports Car or Mini-Van

Outlet Mall or Antiques Shop

Concert or Jazz Bar

Opera or Play

Pool or Darts

Inside or Outside

Grill out or Take-out

Dark Chocolate or Milk Chocolate

Pizza or Chinese

American cheese or Swiss cheese

White or Wheat Bread

Mayonnaise or Mustard

Cake or Pie

Brownies or Cupcakes

Diamonds or Pearls

Earrings or Bracelet

Game Boards or Electronics

Cards or Dominoes

Golf or Basketball

Baseball or Football

Snow or Beach

Book or Magazine

Christian Music or Rock

Country Music or Soul

Book or Bath

Flowers or Candles

Bath scents: Vanilla or Floral

Wheels: Chrome or Alloy

Cologne or Spray

Golf or Fishing

Family Photograph or Painting

Lotion or Body Gel

TV or Movie

Favorite Foods and Restaurants
Favorite Restaurants, directions and phone numbers

Fancy

1. _____

2. _____

3. _____

4. _____

5. _____

Casual

1. _____
2. _____
3. _____
4. _____
5. _____

Take-out favorites

Pizza _____
Chinese _____
Italian _____
BBQ _____
Mexican _____

Top 5 take-out restaurants

1. _____
2. _____
3. _____
4. _____
5. _____

Favorite fast food

Taco Bell _____
Wendy's _____
McDonalds _____
1. _____
2. _____
3. _____
4. _____
5. _____

Favorite Candy

1._____
2._____
3._____
4._____
5._____

Time to Myself
If I had a day in, I would like:

To be by myself _____

Lie around and do nothing _____

A home project _____

1._____
2._____
3._____
4._____

If I had time to myself I would like to:

Take a bath _____

Read a book _____

Sleep in _____

I would love breakfast in bed or breakfast ready.

My favorite breakfast is:

1._____
2._____
3._____
4._____
5._____

If I had a Day Out, I would like to Shop for:

Antiques _____

Houses _____

Cars _____

1. _____

2. _____

3. _____

4. _____

5. _____

Special Things I Love:

1. _____

2. _____

3. _____

4. _____

5. _____

6. _____

7. _____

8. _____

9. _____

10. _____

Jewelry — It's all about the bling!

Jewelry Choices

Earring

1. _____

2. _____

Bracelet

1._____

2._____

Necklace

1._____

2._____

Ring

1._____

2._____

I like

Gold or Silver   Diamonds or Pearls

1._____

2._____

3._____

Favorite Jewelry Stores

1._____
2._____
3._____
4._____
5._____

Vacations

If I could go on vacations I would like:

Snow   Beach   Mountains   Wine country

1._____

2._____

3._____

If I could go on a weekend getaway

In town (see local hotels) _____

Within 100 miles _____

Within 200 miles _____

Things to pack for me:

Clothes _____

Make-up _____

Cleansers _____

Hair Products _____

Miscellaneous must-haves

1._____

2._____

3._____

Destination Ideas

Hawaii	France	Italy
Las Vegas	The Bahamas	Quebec
Mexico	Martha's Vineyard	Oregon
Florida	Colorado	Greece

My Favorite Destinations

1._____

2._____

3._____

4._____

5._____

Favorite Local Hotels

Spa, heated pool, restaurant, or bar. Directions and phone numbers.

1._____

2._____

3._____

4._____

5._____

"Love does magical things to a woman!"

Stephanie Anderson

My Wish List
(Write in pencil & update frequently)

1._____

2._____

3._____

4._____

5._____

6._____

7._____

8._____

9._____

10. _____

11._____

12. _____

13. _____

14._____

15. _____

16. _____

17. _____

18. _____

19. _____

20. _____

*"Love is Learning to Give
even when You Want to Receive!"*

"Love is Complimenting, Not Criticizing."

*"Breath often,
Love will take Your Breathe Away!"*

Question & Answers

This chapter is for fun. Just some crazy questions to help you know her a little better. Take the information, have fun, and add some of your own questions. Or better yet, ask her to journal a little about herself.

What was the happiest day of your life?
_____

Have you ever met a celebrity? Who?
_____

If you could do any job in the world, what would you do?
_____

If you could change anything about yourself, what would it be?
_____

What's your favorite memory?
_____

What's your favorite music?

_____

Do you have a favorite band?

_____

What's your most beloved possession?

_____

What's your favorite movie?

_____

If you had a million dollars, what would you do with it?

_____

Who is the sexiest actor to you?

_____

What was your favorite love scene in a movie?

_____

What's your favorite love song?

_____

If you could change places with anyone, who would it be and why?

_____

If you could eat only one food for the rest of your life, what would
it be?

_____

What is your favorite animal?

_____

If you could have any animal for a pet, what would it be?

_____

What person do you admire the most?

_____

Who was your favorite school teacher?

_____

What's the most romantic date you have ever had?

_____

What is the funniest memory you have?

_____

Where was your fist kiss, and with who?

_____

What was the most embarrassing moment of your life?

_____

What is your favorite sports team?

_____

Did you play sports as a kid? If yes, what kind?

_____

Did you ever want to be a superstar? When and why?

_____

As a kid, who did you want to marry ?

_____

Do you believe in God?

_____

Do you believe in angels?

_____

Would you like to travel into outer space?

_____

If you could have any car you wanted, what would it be?

_____

Who is your favorite family member, and why?

_____

Who do you think taught you the most?

_____

What would you change if you were president?

_____

I really like when you wear your hair:
- ♥ Curly   ♥ Straight
- ♥ Short   ♥ Long

I like when you wear:
   ♥ A suit   ♥ Shorts   ♥ Jeans   ♥ _____

I think you're sexy when you_____

I like when you_____

Your greatest strength to me is_____

When I look at you, I remember what made me fall in love

with you: _____

5 things I love about my guy:

1._____

2._____

3._____

4._____

5._____

You make me smile when you: _____

The best kiss you ever gave me was: _____

I wish you said _____more.

My favorite gift you gave me was: _____

I love the little things you do for me like: _____

I would love to travel to_____

Id like to retire in or on_____

I am (put hearts around the ones that apply)
    ♥ messy
    ♥ clean
    ♥ loud
    ♥ quiet
    ♥ silly
    ♥ serious
    ♥ competitive
    ♥ free-spirited

Favorite movie quote: _____

Favorite movies: _____

What I love about them: _____

When I watch them I feel:_____

I always cry when I watch: _____

I always laugh when I watch: _____

Favorite TV shows: _____

What I love about them: _____

72

Favorite books: _____

Favorite snack food: _____

♥ Morning _____

♥ Night_____

♥ Bedtime snack_____

Favorite games_____

Favorite holiday_____

I love the smell of
    ♥ in my home _____
    ♥ cologne _____
    ♥ perfume _____
    ♥ lotion _____
    ♥ bath scent _____

I love weather when it is
    ♥ cold
    ♥ hot
    ♥ rainy
    ♥ snow

Favorite cartoon as a kid_____
Favorite commercial: _____
My hidden talent: _____

One of my favorite dates with you was: _____

Our most romantic date: _____

Our most unusual date: _____

Our worst date: _____

Every time I hear this song_____I think of you

Places I love to shop: _____

My favorite color: _____

Number: _____

Hobbies: _____

Names, addresses, and e-mails
Directions and phone numbers:

Babysitters

1._____

2._____

3._____

Family

Mom _____

Dad _____

Sister(s) _____

Brother(s) _____

Grandpa _____

Grandma _____

In-laws

Mom _____

Dad _____

Sister(s) _____

Brother (s) _____

Grandpa _____

Grandma _____

My Best Girlfriends

1. _____
2. _____
3. _____
4. _____
5. _____
6. _____
7. _____
8. _____
9. _____
10. _____

"True Girlfriends are One in A Million."

"All Girls Need a Good Girlfriend!"

Important Numbers
To Know

What other contacts are important for your guy to have?
Add them below:

1. _____

2. _____

3. _____

4. _____

5. _____

6. _____

7. _____

8. _____

9. _____

10. _____

Her Journal

His Journal

# Notes

Use these pages for capturing important facts about your lady. When you hear her say she would like to have or do something, this is where you write it down. Record those wishes and make them come true.

When you go shopping, take this book with you. It now holds all the important info you need to know for delighting your lover. No more puzzling over what she might like or what will fit. You should be able to find the answers in these pages.

Notes

Notes

Notes

Notes

Notes

Notes

CPSIA information can be obtained
at www.ICGtesting.com
Printed in the USA
FSOW02n0952250216
17282FS